MW01069521

Who Is the Antichrist?

Michael Pearl

International Bestselling Author of *GOOD AND EVIL*

Publication date: April 2016

Print: ISBN: 978-1-61644-087-9
ePub: ISBN: 978-1-61644-088-6
ePDF: ISBN: 978-1-61644-089-3

All Scripture quotations are taken from the King James Holy Bible

Library of Congress Control Number: 2016900927

All Bible references are taken from the common text received through Greek, Latin, and multiple Indo-European languages and preserved in every generation since the first century down to the present, otherwise known as the Received Text, whose sole representative in the English language is commonly known as the King James Bible.

1. Antichrist 2. Rapture 3. End Times 4. Revelation 5. The Beast
6. Second Coming 7. Apocalypse 8. Prophecy
I. Pearl, Michael II. Who Is the Antichrist?

Who Is the Antichrist? may be purchased at special quantity discounts for churches, donor programs, fund raising, book clubs, or educational purposes for churches, congregations, schools and universities. Rights and Licensing in other languages and international sales opportunities are available. For more information contact:

Mel Cohen • 1000 Pearl Road • Pleasantville TN 37033
(931) 593-2484 • mcohen@nogreaterjoy.org

Cover design by Megan Van Vuren
Interior layout by Michael Pearl & Aaron Aprile
Printed in the United States of America

Publisher: No Greater Joy Ministries, Inc.
www.nogreaterjoy.org

TABLE OF CONTENTS

FOREWORD

One of the most misunderstood doctrines of Scripture concerns antichrist, due mainly to the many popular books and movies on the subject. If one were to write an accurate novel that covered the tribulation period, it would not be a pleasant read. There would be no love stories, no second chances, no one getting "born again," no heroes fighting the antichrist system and surviving.

In reality, the many Christian books and movies have actually prepared the way for antichrist to deceive the world into thinking that he is the Christ. The biblical facts concerning antichrist are far different from popular belief. This little book will point you in the right direction and launch your study of this critical subject.

CHAPTER 1
Nature of Antichrist

Antichrist is not about a mark, rather about a religious figurehead and his ministry. Popular preoccupation with his number has obscured his nature.

Defining Antichrist

Most people think that antichrist is someone who is against Christ, as in a godless, secular ruler. To the contrary, the final antichrist aspires to be Christ and presents himself to the world as God. He seeks worship. He only persecutes those who will not believe in him.

The English prefix *anti-* dates all the way back through the European languages to Latin and Greek (ἀντί), where it is spelled and pronounced exactly as it is in English today. Greek lexicons bear out what is more than abundantly obvious in our English Bible.

> *anti-*
> in place of, replacement, substitution

Greek Dictionary of the New Testament

ἀντί, anti, an-tee´; a prim. particle; opposite, i.e., instead or because of (rarely in addition to):—for, in the room of. Often used in composition to denote contrast, requital, substitution, correspondence, etc.

Strong's Greek Lexicon

ἀντί [anti] is one of the prepositions whose use goes back to the Hellenistic period. In its basic meaning of "over against" . . . is mostly used in the sense of a. "in place of," . . . In this respect it makes little difference whether the word denotes an actual replacement, an intended replacement, or a mere equivalent in estimation.

Antichrist is another christ "in place of" Jesus Christ. He offers himself "instead of, in the room of" the Lord Jesus Christ. *Anti*-christ is opposed to Christ only in the sense that he claims the title for himself. He offers himself as the object of worship (Revelation 13:6, 15), and presents himself in the temple in Jerusalem as the true Messiah (2 Thessalonians 2:4) come to bring peace to the world. His offer is universal to all religions (Revelation 13:16).

Many Antichrists

The designation "antichrist" is not reserved for that one, end-time person. Even before Jesus was revealed to the world there were antichrists (Acts 5:36–37).

The New Testament church was already plagued by antichrists. "Little children, it is the last time: and as ye have heard that antichrist **shall** come, even now are there **many antichrists;** whereby we know that it is the last time" (1 John 2:18).

One Final Antichrist

Note that while saying that there are "many" antichrists (plural), he also says, "we know that antichrist *[singular]* **shall come.**" The first-century church had been taught that a single personality would mark "the last time" just as the prophet Daniel had revealed 500 years earlier. The end-time apocalyptic figure called antichrist is not the first, but he will be the last. Ever since the first century, without fail the church has been continuously plagued with antichrists, each typifying the final antichrist to come in the last days.

The Doctrine of Antichrist

Antichrists are marked by a particular doctrine.

> **1 John 4:3**
> And every spirit that confesseth not that Jesus Christ is come in the flesh is not of God: and this is that spirit of antichrist, whereof ye have heard that it *[spirit of antichrist]* should come *[future]*; and **even now already is it in the world** *[the spirit of antichrist is in the world]*.

The "spirit of antichrist" is seen in denying that Jesus is God come in the flesh. Mormons, Jehovah's Witnesses, and any so-called Christian sect that denies that Jesus is the one and only God, creator of heaven and earth, come to the earth in human flesh, is antichrist.

The spirit of antichrist is seen in denying that Jesus is God come in the flesh.

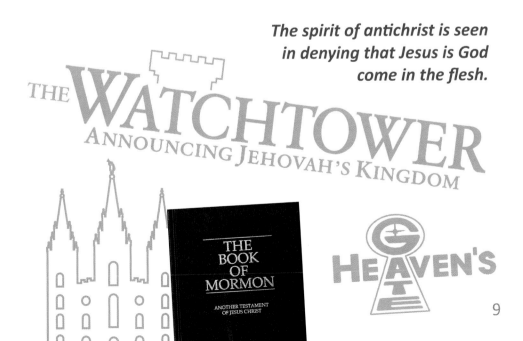

9

Note the Word: *Anti-christ*

Antichrist is not anti-Allah or anti-Buddha, nor even anti-God or anti-religion. He is anti-Christ. **The antichrist movement will be a Christian movement.** No doubt antichrist will utilize the Bible, just as does the Mormon Church. To complete his deception, it seems reasonable that antichrist will profess to believe in the inspiration of the Bible in its original autographs, but he will not believe in its preservation in any language, for he will have observed how effective that has been in permitting the introduction and acceptance of divergent doctrines of devils.

> **Mark 13:22**
> For false Christs and false prophets shall rise, and shall shew signs and wonders, to seduce, if it were possible, even the elect.

Since all of the prophecies in the Bible concerning events that have now become history were fulfilled in a literal manner, then we are quite comfortable in expecting all prophecies of future events to be fulfilled

in precisely the same manner. The Bible guarantees as much. And God stakes his reputation on it as revealed in the following passage.

Isaiah 46:9–11

9 Remember the former things of old: for I am God, and there is none else; I am God, and there is none like me,

10 Declaring the end from the beginning, and from ancient times the things that are not yet done, saying, My counsel shall stand, and I will do all my pleasure:

11[b] Yea, I have spoken it, I will also bring it to pass; I have purposed it, I will also do it.

> **The antichrist movement will be a Christian movement.**

CHAPTER 2
The Word *Antichrist* Appears in the Bible Five Times

This will be an overview of all references to antichrist. The distinguishing characteristics of antichrists are highlighted in bold text.

First three uses of word antichrist

1 John 2:18–19, 22–23
18 Little children, it is the last time: and as ye have heard that **antichrist shall come,** even now are there **many antichrists;** whereby we know that it is **the last time.**
19 They *[plural]* **went out from us,** but they were **not of us;** for if they had been of us, they would no doubt have continued with us: but they went out, that they might be made manifest that they were not all of us.

Seven uses of *they* confirm the plurality of antichrists in a single generation.

22 Who is a liar but he that denieth that Jesus is the Christ? He is antichrist, that denieth the Father and the Son. *[a definition of the doctrine of antichrist]*

23 Whosoever denieth the Son, the same hath not the Father: (but) he that acknowledgeth the Son hath the Father also.

Antichrist denies the deity of the Son while attempting to acknowledge the Father. It is the Father-Son relationship that he denies—the godhead, the trinity.

Points gleaned from the above passage:

- Antichrist (singular) "shall come" at "the last time." So his coming is future.
- It is someone who was counted among the Christians (1 John 2:19).
- But he is not a true Christian (1 John 2:19).
- He goes out from the believers (1 John 2:19).
- He denies that Jesus is the Christ (1 John 2:22) but not the concept of a Christ.
- He denies the unity of the Father and the Son—non-trinitarian (1 John 2:22–23).
- He denies that Jesus Christ is come in the flesh (1 John 4:3; 2 John 7).

Summary of 1 John 2:18–23

Antichrist is a **man** who leaves the fellowship of believers, denying that Jesus and the Father are one and denying that Jesus is God's son—the Christ in human flesh.

Antichrist denies "the Father and the Son" (1 John 2:22)—the equality of the Son with the Father. He attempts to elevate the Father alone, which is to denigrate the Son.

Fourth of five uses of word antichrist

1 John 4:1–6

1 Beloved, **believe not every spirit,** but try the spirits whether they are of God: because many **false prophets** are gone out into the world. *[Antichrist is a false PROPHET.]*
2 Hereby know ye the Spirit of God: Every spirit that **confesseth that Jesus Christ is come in the flesh** is of God: *[Antichrist will deny the incarnation.]*
3 And **every spirit that confesseth not that Jesus Christ is come in the flesh is not of God: and this is that spirit of <u>antichrist</u>,** whereof ye have heard that it should come; and even **now already is it in the world.**

This is a clear statement as to the essence of antichrist doctrine and motivation.

4 **Ye are of God, little children, and have overcome them: because greater is he that is in you, than he that is in the world.**
5 They are of the world: therefore speak they of the world, and the world heareth them.
6 We are of God: he that knoweth God heareth us; he that is not of God heareth not us. Hereby know we the spirit of truth, and the **spirit of error.**

Summary of 1 John 4:1–7

- Antichrist is a "false prophet."
- He is a "deceiver."
- He is the "spirit of error."
- Denies that "Jesus is come in the flesh."

Fifth of five uses of word antichrist

2 John 7–11

7 For many deceivers are entered into the world, who **confess not that Jesus Christ is come in the flesh.** This is a **deceiver** and an <u>**antichrist.**</u>
8 Look to yourselves, that we lose not those things which we have wrought, but that we receive a full reward.
9 Whosoever transgresseth, and **abideth not in the doctrine of Christ,** hath not God. He that abideth in the doctrine of Christ, he hath both the Father and the Son.

Here is redundant confirmation of the nature of antichrist. He denies the son while attempting to promote the Father.

10 If there come any unto you, and bring not this doctrine, receive him not into your house, neither bid him God speed:
11 For he that biddeth him God speed is partaker of his evil deeds.

Summary of 2 John 7–11

Once again we have a clear definition of the nature of antichrist doctrine.

- He does not "confess that Jesus Christ is come in the flesh."
- He does not "abide in the doctrine of Christ."
- He is called a "deceiver" because he is not just a person who fails to believe; rather, he is active in proclaiming his doctrine of disbelief.

Key verse exposing antichrist doctrine

1 John 5:7
For there are three that bear record in heaven, the Father, the Word, and the Holy Ghost: and these **three are one.**

This one biblical passage is completely disconcerting to all antichrists. In keeping with the spirit of antichrist, this passage has been removed from all commercial Bible versions with the exception of the NKJV, where its authenticity is questioned in the margin. What does it say

> Antichrist denies the deity of the Son while attempting to acknowledge the Father.

regarding deception when the most powerful verse in the Bible supporting the very thing antichrist denies is removed by modern Bible critics? The Bible correctors and those who use their corrupted products are

promoting "the spirit of antichrist," and will have a part in deceiving the world when the man of sin does make his appearance. See my work on 1 John 5:7 where I show how the Scripture supports the inclusion of this text.

Key:

> **The Antichrist will cause people to WANT to believe his lies.**

CHAPTER 3
Other Names for Antichrist

The end-time antichrist has other names that are quite descriptive and broaden our understanding of his origin, nature, and reign. Each name is emphasized with a bullet arrow.

The prophet Daniel had a lot to say about end-time events and the personality that would dominate. These references deserve—yea, demand—a much more thorough examination in their contexts if one is to appreciate the definitiveness of each, but space and the reader's patience will not allow. My commentary will make occasional assertions for which I offer no proof beyond the obvious sense of the text. Some conclusions will be based on multiple texts that we will not take the space to review. There is an abundance of material online that addresses these passages in an accurate manner. The reader who wants better support will need to do further independent research. This work is designed to provide you with a simple overview of the Scripture on the subject of antichrist.

> ➤ *Little Horn (a name of antichrist found in Daniel)*

A Summary of What You Will Read in Daniel

Daniel was a captive in Babylon in the sixth century BC. God revealed to the prophet the future of Israel and the nations that would impact Israel down to the end of the world. Daniel saw four mountain-top, prominent kingdoms in their succession: Babylon (during Daniel's tenure), Medo Persia (which Daniel lived to see), and later Greece and its four divisions (with details of the rivalry of the Ptolemy and Seleucid divisions recorded in Daniel 11), followed by the fourth kingdom that would not be as glorious but would be exceptionally powerful. Time would reveal it to be the Roman Empire. The first three kingdoms were represented as beasts: lion, bear, and leopard. The fourth kingdom, Roman, was represented as a beast as well, but it would be a mechanical beast made of iron and brass and would be more powerful than the three kingdoms before it.

Daniel 7:7

After this I saw in the night visions, and behold a fourth beast, dreadful and terrible, and strong exceedingly; and it had great iron teeth: it devoured and brake in pieces, and stamped the residue with the feet of it: and it was diverse from all the beasts that were before it; and it had **ten horns.**

The fourth beast, Rome, is represented as having **ten horns.** The angel tells us that the ten horns are **"ten kings that shall arise"** (Daniel 7:24).

In the vision of the metallic beast, Daniel sees a **little horn** (Daniel 7:8) rise up among the ten horns, and the angel informs him that "another shall rise after them; and he shall be diverse from the first, and he shall subdue three kings" (Daniel 7:24). **That little horn is antichrist.**

After the four beasts and the last-days, ten-state division with the little horn gaining dominance, a final kingdom, represented as a rock, rolls down the mountain and smashes all the kingdoms into oblivion and then grows to become a mountain kingdom itself. That final kingdom is the Kingdom of Heaven.

The Scripture Concerning the Little Horn (Antichrist)

We will now review the Scripture in Daniel that speaks of the little horn.

> **Daniel 7:8–10**
> **8** I considered the horns, and, behold, there came up among them another **little horn,** before whom there were three of the first horns *[horns are rulers of nations—Daniel 7:24]* plucked up by the roots: and, behold, in this horn were eyes like the eyes of **man,** and a **mouth speaking great things** *[antichrist]*.

This is an account of antichrist in the last days, conquering three of the ten nations that had been incorporated into the old **Roman Empire.**

21

9 I beheld till the thrones were cast down *[nations and their rulers defeated at the second coming of Christ]*, and the Ancient of days did sit *[on his throne in the millennium]*, whose garment was white as snow, and the hair of his head like the pure wool: his throne was like the fiery flame, and his wheels as burning fire.

10 A fiery stream issued and came forth from before him: thousand thousands *[millions]* ministered unto him, and ten thousand times ten thousand *[one hundred million survivors of the*

tribulation] stood before him: the judgment was set, and the books were opened *[the judgment of nations at the beginning of the millennium— Matthew 25:32].*

Timeframe

Notice how this ruler called the **"little horn" arises right before, and reigns until, the Ancient of days opens the books to judge the world.** This happens at the end of the tribulation. You will need to read the greater context of Daniel 7 to fully appreciate the text.

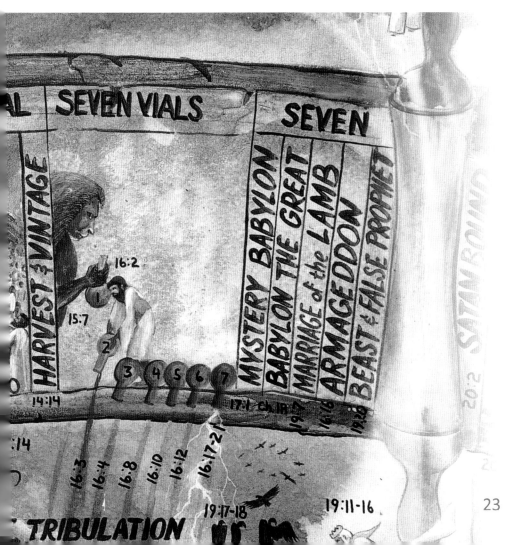

Mouth Speaking Great Things

Also notice that antichrist is characterized as a "mouth speaking great things." He is a charismatic leader attempting to move the entire world to worship him.

- He is a ruler that gains control of three other nations (and eventually ten).
- He is a man.
- He speaks great things.
- He is active until the Ancient of days sits on his throne—that is until the beginning of the millennium.
- He is judged by Jesus Christ.

Daniel 7:25
And he shall **speak great words** against the most High, and shall **wear out the saints of the most High,** and think to **change times and laws:** and they shall be given into his hand until a **time** and **times** and the **dividing of time.**

Four things are revealed in this one verse. This "little horn" that gains ascendency over the ten horns will:

- "Speak great words against the most High."
- "Wear out the saints of the most High." He will persecute the Jews that remain on the earth after the rapture (Revelation 12:5–17).
- "Think to change times and laws."
- Be prominent for just three and one half years.

Antichrist (Little Horn) Tries to Change Times and Laws

This is a fascinating prophecy—that antichrist will make an attempt to "change times and laws."

> **Daniel 7:25**
> And he shall . . . think to change **times and laws** . . . .

What are the "times" he thinks to change? The best commentary on the Bible is the Bible itself. If you are reading in English, that would be the Authorized Version, of course. So we will do a little Bible research to learn what God means when he speaks of a "time."

Nature and Length of a "Time"

The term *time* is used in prophecy to reference a Jewish year of 360 days composed of twelve 30-day lunar months. The book of Daniel uses the word *time/s* twelve times in the same manner (2:21; 4:16 (360-day year), 7:12, 25; 12:7); and the book of Revelation uses it three times (Revelation 12:14), reflecting Daniel's use.

The three and one-half years of the tribulation is referenced as "time, and times, and a half time" (Revelation 12:14), and as 1260 days (Revelation 11:3; 12:6), and as 42 months (Revelation 11:2; 13:5).

So we know "time" is one 360-day year. "Times" is two years. And "a half time" is one-half year. So 3½ Jewish years of 360 days each is 42 months, or 1260 days, the length of the latter half of the seven-year period known as "Jacob's trouble" (Jeremiah 30:7). There is no contest on that point. It is well established in the text and in the consensus of exegeses.

Jewish times are based on Jewish laws. All of the feast days, Sabbaths, and sacrifices are based on the Jewish calendar.

25

Why Times and Not Years?

So why does the Bible go to such extents to emphasize a 360-day time composed of twelve 30-day months? Note that it doesn't call the 360-day *time* a year, because when Israel added a thirteenth month to make up for the 4½-day deficit, a year would be longer than 360 days, for it would be composed of thirteen moon cycles instead of twelve. With our Gregorian calendar there is no way to specify how many days are in a six-month period without specifying which months in which years, since the number of days in a month varies from 28 to 31. The number of days in a year varies even more in a leap year. So it is that no solar or lunar calendar is capable of specifying the exact number of days in a randomly chosen three-and-one-half-year span. But prophecy is exact. That exactness is maintained by referencing *times* instead of years. A time composed of twelve 30-day months is always 360 days according to any calendar.

Antichrist Seeks to Change Laws

The text links **times** with **laws.** So we have another clue with which to sleuth an interpretation. We must seek to answer how the changing of *laws* will aid in the changing of *times,* or vice versa. Jewish times are based on Jewish laws. All of the feast days, Sabbaths, and sacrifices are based on the Jewish calendar, and the calendar is always based on the moon. The law commands them to observe certain ceremonial events and sacrifices on the same day (moon cycle) every year.

> **Genesis 1:14**
> And God said, Let there be lights in the firmament of the heaven to divide the day from the night; and let them be for signs, and for seasons, and for **days, and years.**

We are told in Genesis 1:16–18 that the sun and moon are given to "rule the day" and to "rule the night."

To change the *times* would be to change the *laws* governing Jewish holy days and Sabbaths. Obviously, antichrist is not going to be able to change the moon cycles, so the only thing left is for him to change the Scripture regarding the coordination of holy days with the moon cycles. It could be that in his feigned role as God, he will demand that the Jewish holy days be observed according to the Gregorian calendar that the Western world uses rather than the "outdated" Jewish calendar.

But the text says he will **"think"** to change times and laws, indicating he will fail in his attempt.

It is not essential that we know for certain what it means to change the times and laws, for those who are living upon the earth when antichrist makes an effort to change the times and laws will reference this passage and know that there is a God in Israel who knows the end from the beginning.

He will "think" to change times indicates he will fail in his attempt.

➤ *A King of Fierce Countenance*
(a name of antichrist)

Daniel 8:23–25

23 And in the latter time of their kingdom, when the transgressors are come to the full, a king of **fierce countenance, and understanding dark sentences** *[difficult to understand speech]*, shall stand up *[his political position predates his "standing up"]*.
24 And his **power shall be mighty,** but not by his own power: and he shall **destroy wonderfully,** and shall **prosper,** and **practise,** and shall **destroy the mighty and the holy people.**
25 And through his **policy** also he shall cause **craft to prosper in his hand;** and he shall **magnify himself in his heart,** and **by peace shall destroy many:** he shall also **stand up against the Prince of princes; but he shall be broken without hand.**

- A king—he is a political power, ruler of a nation before he is manifested as antichrist.
- Of fierce countenance—he has a powerful, captivating presence.
- Understanding dark secrets—he has the ability to decipher complex speech.
- His power shall be mighty—high level of power.

- Destroy wonderfully—his level of destruction will be amazing.
- Prosper—in his endeavors.
- Practice—he will put into operation what he intends.
- Destroy the mighty and holy people—the Jews.
- He will be in a position to form policy.
- Through his policies he will cause craft (the art of deceitfulness) to prosper.
- He will magnify himself in his heart— he will think more highly of himself than he ought.
- In the guise of bringing peace to the world he will destroy many.
- He will stand up against the Prince of princes, Jesus Christ.
- He will be broken by Jesus Christ without Christ so much as lifting his hand.

➤ Man of Sin *(a name of antichrist)*

2 Thessalonians 2:1–6
1 Now we beseech you, brethren, by the coming of our Lord Jesus Christ *[Second Coming]*, and by our gathering together unto him *[Rapture]*,
2 That ye be not soon shaken in mind, or be troubled, neither by spirit, nor by word, nor by letter as from us, as that the day of Christ is at hand.

"For that day shall not come, except there come a falling away first..."

Paul tells them that he has not written anything or spoken anything, nor has he indicated with his spirit that the day of Christ was about to take place, for before Christ returns there will be a falling away from the faith and antichrist will be revealed to the world.

> **3** Let no man deceive you by any means: for that day shall not come, except there come a **falling away first,** and that **man of sin** be revealed, the **son of perdition** [discussed later];
>
> **4** Who **opposeth** [opposes Jesus Christ] and **exalteth himself above** all that is called God, or that is worshipped; so that **he as God sitteth in the temple of God, shewing himself that he is God.**
>
> **5** Remember ye not, that, when I was yet with you, I told you these things?
>
> **6** And now ye know what withholdeth that he might be revealed in his time.

- He is the man of sin.
- He opposes all deities.
- He will not come until there is a general falling away from the faith.

- He will be manifested to the world prior to the Second Coming.
- He exalts himself above the god of every religion and above every object of worship.
- He will sit in the Jewish temple as a means to show the world that he is the God of the Jews and of the whole world.

Though antichrist will deceive the world, in time he will be revealed as the man of sin. In contrast, we know Jesus as "Jesus Christ the righteous." Sin will be the essence of antichrist's heart; it will be his practice, his ambition, the primary product of his short reign, and it will be his end.

➤ *The Wicked (a name of antichrist)*

2 Thessalonians 2:8–12
8 And then shall that **Wicked** be revealed, whom the Lord shall consume with the spirit of his mouth, and shall destroy with the brightness of his coming: **9** Even him, whose coming is **after the working of Satan** with all **power and signs and lying wonders,** **10** And with all **deceivableness** of unrighteousness in them that perish; because they received not the love of the truth, that they might be saved.

11 And for this cause God shall send them strong delusion, that they should believe a lie: **12** That they all might be damned who believed not the truth, but had pleasure in unrighteousness.

- Antichrist is named **Wicked.** He is the personification of all that is wicked and devilish.
- Satan enables him to come into the world.
- Satan enables him to possess all kinds of power witnessed by public signs and wonders and lying miracles.
- He comes with ALL deceivableness in regard to those who perish. They will think he is something other than his true nature. They will be surprised to learn that he is a fake, a liar, and a deceiver.

➢ *The Mystery of Iniquity*
(a name of antichrist)

2 Thessalonians 2:7
For the **mystery of iniquity** doth already work: only he who now letteth will let, until he be taken out of the way.

In the Bible the word *mystery* is used to refer to something God has deliberately hidden from the majority but revealed in part to the wise. Antichrist is a man of sin and iniquity in a sense that is yet a mystery to us. Apparently his relationship to the devil is unique.

Certainly he has supernatural powers to do miracles (Revelation 13:13—note the numbers), so he is the final, all-out antichrist prophesied by God and prepared by the devil to be the great man of sin. God will even assist him by giving him free reign for a little **13:13** less (Mark 13:20) than 1260 days (Daniel 7:25).

So the nature of antichrist's iniquity is something of a mystery. The mystery will come to light when we examine him as the son of perdition and then as the beast.

Key:

Mystery is used to refer to something God has deliberately hidden from the majority but revealed in part to the wise.

CHAPTER 4
The Son of Perdition

Son of perdition is another name for antichrist. We are going to dedicate an entire chapter to this one title as we try to unravel the mystery. We will likely go where you have never gone before. If you read something bizarre, welcome to the world of Bible mysteries.

➢ *The Son of Perdition (a name of antichrist)*

2 Thessalonians 2:3
Let no man deceive you by any means: for that day shall not come, except there come a falling away first, and that man of sin be revealed, **the son of perdition** . . .

Antichrist is called *THE* son (not *A* son) of **perdition,** meaning there is just one son of perdition. It is not saying that he is destined to perdition, rather perdition is his place of origin. He is the product of perdition. We will come to an explanation of that in Revelation 17:8 below.

Definition of Perdition

The word *perdition* is used eight times in the English Holy Bible, all in the New Testament. The eight readings provide a very clean and

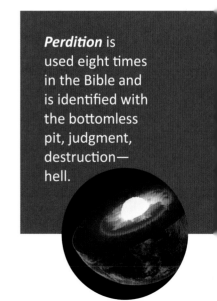

Perdition is used eight times in the Bible and is identified with the bottomless pit, judgment, destruction—hell.

unambiguous definition. Perdition is identified with the bottomless pit, judgment, destruction—hell. Whereas the bottomless pit is a place, perdition is both the place and the state of being damned.

Two Sons of Perdition?

Two of the eight references speak of "the son of perdition," referencing two different individuals, antichrist and Judas, who betrayed Jesus. As strange as it may seem, possibly these two are one. Notice that both are preceded by the definite article *the*.

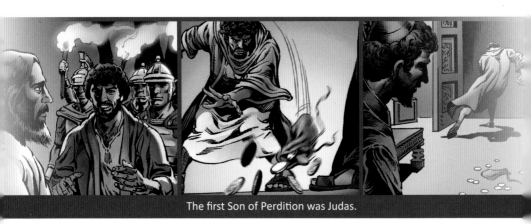

The first Son of Perdition was Judas.

First Son of Perdition—Judas

In the last hours before his crucifixion, when praying to the Father, Jesus celebrated the fact that he had not lost a single person of faith during his entire ministry. Jesus had secured complete safekeeping for all believers, with but one unique exception—the "son of perdition" who went "to his own place" in hell. Jesus seems to imply that Judas was in a unique category, in that his departure was not actually losing any believers, for he was a son of perdition from the beginning, being previously identified with perdition.

John 17:12
While I was with them in the world, I kept them in thy name: those that thou gavest me I have kept, and none of them is lost, but the son of perdition; that the scripture might be fulfilled.

Acts 1:25
That he may take part of this ministry and apostleship, from which Judas by transgression fell, that he might go to his own place.

Second and Last Son of Perdition—Antichrist

Antichrist is also **THE** son of perdition.

2 Thessalonians 2:3–4
3 Let no man deceive you by any means: for that day shall not come, except there come a falling away first, and that man of sin be revealed, **the son of perdition;**
4 Who opposeth and exalteth himself above all that is called God, or that is worshipped; so that he as God sitteth in the temple of God, shewing himself that he is God.

In antichrist, the son of perdition is manifested once again.

- Antichrist is called the son of perdition.
- Antichrist has his origin among the damned in hell.
- His coming will be preceded by a falling away from the faith.
- He will precede the Second Coming.
- He opposes all religions.

- He exalts himself above all gods or objects of worship.
- He will sit in the Jewish temple in Jerusalem as a way of demonstrating that he is God.

Are Judas and Antichrist Both the One Son of Perdition?

I readily admit, I do not know for certain. But the Bible definitely indicates a link. There are only two possibilities.

1) The spirit of Satan dwells in each of them, and so at one time Judas was THE son of perdition, and later, after Judas has died, antichrist is THE son of perdition. That would assume that Scripture is employing hyperbole, which I find difficult. We would have to believe that when Jesus said they were the son of perdition, he actually meant they were so influenced by the devil as to owe their defiant ways to the devil. If that were the case then neither Judas nor antichrist would actually originate in perdition. We would also have to conclude that Jesus was only using colorful language when he said that upon his death, Judas "went to his own place," indicating that hell was previously his home. The Scripture does not employ the terminology *son of perdition* to apply to any other great sinner.
2) The other possibility is that in a way we do not yet understand, the spirit and soul of Judas preexisted in hell and was incarnate in human form. Likewise upon Judas returning to hell, that same spirit awaits in hell to be reincarnated in antichrist. Hang in there; we have just started our investigation into this mystery.

He Was, and Is Not, yet Is, and Shall Be

Revelation 17:8, 10–11
8 The beast that thou sawest **was** *[antichrist preexisted]*, and **is not** *[at the time John wrote, antichrist was not]*; and **shall ascend** *[in the future]* out of the bottomless pit, and go into perdition: and they that dwell on the earth shall wonder, whose names were not written in the book of life from the foundation of the world, when they behold the beast that **was, and is not, and yet is** *[notice that he was and is not at the same time]*. 10 And there are seven kings: five are fallen, and one is, and the other is not yet come; and when he cometh, he must continue a short space. 11 And the beast that **was, and is not,** even he is the eighth, and is of the seven, and goeth into perdition.

Was, Is Not, and Is

John says, ". . . behold the **beast that was, and is not, and yet is.**" The language is clear though the concept is difficult. It is not hard to understand, though it may be hard to believe. It would not be hard to understand if we were watching a science fiction movie. Antichrist was present on the earth before 95 AD, but at the time of the writing he was not on the earth because he was in the bottomless pit. So he **is** though he **is not.** And in the future he will ascend out of the bottomless pit

(Revelation 11:7) where he will take his place as the eighth of seven kings. After 3½ years he will go back into the bottomless pit where he will stay until cast into everlasting hell (Revelation 20:10).

So the concept we are focusing on is the idea that the son of perdition (antichrist) was on the earth prior to John's writing (meaning that would be Judas) but at the time of writing was in the bottomless pit (perdition), and will come out of the pit to once again be active on the earth as the last-days son of perdition, or antichrist.

The link between a preexistent son of perdition, Judas, and antichrist is strong. What to make of it is still open for discussion.

This sounds so strange on so many levels that I have a hard time believing it. But you wanted to know what saith the Scripture. So there it is.

- Antichrist existed prior to John's writing.
- Antichrist was not (upon the earth at the time of writing).
- Yet antichrist was in the bottomless pit (perdition) at the time of writing.
- He will ascend out of the bottomless pit at a later date (Revelation 11:7).
- He will be the eighth of seven kings.

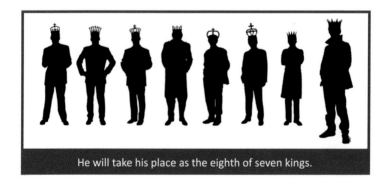

He will take his place as the eighth of seven kings.

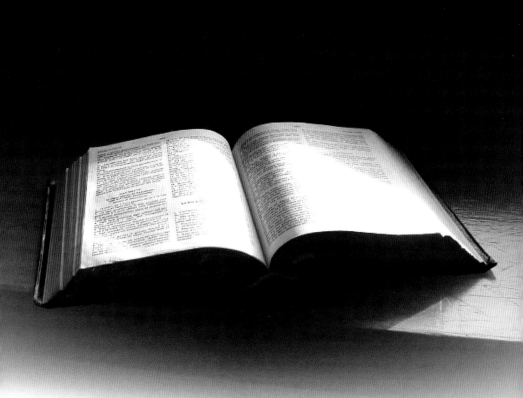

Don't Give Up

Those who are new to Bible study will no doubt find this a bit overwhelming and may feel like giving up. But with persistent study it becomes less confusing, and in time it will all make perfect sense, though some things may remain a mystery. If fact, in response to this subject, the angel tells John that the nature of the beast is meant to be a **mystery** (Revelation 17:7). We need a book to reveal these things to us. Perhaps the book could be named Revelation.

Key:

> **During this time it is easy to be deceived.**

instruments of musicke: nei-
|| brought before him, and his sleepe went
from him.

19 Then the king arose very early
in the morning, and went in haste vnto
the den of Lyons.

20 And when he came to the den, he
cryed with a lamentable voice vnto
Daniel, and the king spake and said to
Daniel: O Daniel, seruant of the liuing
God, Is thy God whom thou seruest
continually, able to deliuer thee from
the Lyons?

21 Then said Daniel vnto the king,
O king, liue for euer.

22 My God hath sent his Angel, and
hath shut the lyons mouthes that they
haue not hurt me: forasmuch as before
him, innocencie was found in me; and
also before thee, O king, haue I done
no hurt.

23 Then was the king exceeding
glad for him, and commanded that they
should take Daniel vp out of the denne:
Daniel was taken vp out of the den,
d no maner of hurt was found vpon
n, because he beleeued in his God.

24 ¶ And the king commanded, and
y brought those men which had ac-
d Daniel, and they cast them into the
of Lyons, them, their children, and
wiues: and the Lyons had the
ery of them, and brake all their
s in pieces or euer they came at the
me of the den.

¶ Then king Darius wrote vn-
eople, nations, and languages
well in all the earth; Peace be
lied vnto you.

I make a decree, That in euery
n of my kingdome, men trem-
eare before the God of Daniel:
he liuing God, and stedfast for
his kingdome that, which shal
estroyed, and his dominion
n vnto the end.

deliuereth and rescueth, and
h signes and wonders in hea
earth: Who hath

N the first yee
chazzar king of
Daniel † had a dr
visions of his h
his bed: then he
dreame, and tolde the summ
|| matters.

2 Daniel spake, and said, S
my vision by night, & behold, t
windes of the heauen stroue vp
great Sea.

3 And foure great beastes ca
from the sea, diuers one from anc

4 The first was like a Lyo
had Eagles Wings: I beheld ti
wings thereof were pluckt, || and i
lifted vp from the earth, and made
vpon the feete as a man, and a n
heart was giuen to it.

5 And behold, another beast,
cond, like to a Beare, and || it raise
it selfe on one side, and it had three rib
in the mouth of it betweene the teeth
it, and they said thus vnto it, Arise,
uoure much flesh.

6 After this I beheld, and loe, an
ther like a Leopard, which had vpo
the backe of it foure wings of a foul
the beast had also foure heads, and do
minion was giuen to it.

7 After this I saw in the night vi
sions, and behold, a fourth beast, dread-
ly; and it had great yron teeth: it deuou-
red and brake in pieces, and stamped the
residue with the feete of it, and it was diuers from all the beasts that were before
it, and it had ten hornes.

8 I considered the hornes, and behold, there came vp among them another little horne, before whom there
were three of the first hornes pluckt vp
by the roots; and behold, in this horne
were eyes like the eyes of man, and a
mouth speaking great things.

9 ¶ I beheld till the thrones were
cast downe, and the Ancient of dayes
did sit, whose garment was white as
snow, and the haire

CHAPTER 5
Why Is Antichrist Called a Beast?

He is not called a beast because he is animal-like or beastly in nature. It is a well-established biblical metaphor common in prophecy, the meaning of which is not in question.

The Beasts of Daniel

The book of Daniel is the place to start in our investigation of the meaning of the prophetic beast. The book of Revelation reflects Daniel. Daniel and Revelation are like the prequel and sequel, respectively, of a trilogy, the gospels lying between them.

The book of Daniel uses the word *beast/s* in a prophetic sense 11 times (the number of dissolution). Revelation uses the word *beast/s* in the same manner 37 times. That is 48 times in these two prophetic books. These 48

The Received Text in any language defines its own terms.

references are absolutely consistent in their symbolism. We don't need to guess about the meaning. We actually have an angel's definitive statement regarding the meaning of the word *beast*.

The symbolic use began with visions God gave the prophet Daniel in the sixth century BC. God also gave him the interpretation of the visions.

Daniel's Vision Is an Outline of World History as It Affects Israel

Daniel 7:2–9

2 Daniel spake and said, I saw in my vision by night, and, behold, the four winds of the heaven [*nations*] strove upon the great sea [*the world*].

The meaning of "the four winds of heaven" and the great "sea" are determined by reviewing every usage of these words in prophetic writings in the English language. Of course if Greek or Hebrew are your native tongues then you will find the same amazing consistency in them. The Received Text in any language defines its own terms. We never need to guess.

Conflict of Nations from Daniel to the First Century

3 And four great beasts came up from the sea [*world*], diverse one from another.

Later in the text, the angel tells Daniel that the four beasts represent **four kings** and their **kingdoms**. Native characteristics of the animals are matched with characteristics of the kings they represent and with recognized national symbols.

The first was like a lion, and had eagle's wings.

The First Beast
Babylon and Nebuchadnezzar (625–538 BC)

> **4 The first was like a lion, and had eagle's wings: I beheld till the wings thereof were plucked, and it was lifted up from the earth, and made stand upon the feet as a man, and a man's heart was given to it.**

Archeologists have identified as many as **120 lions** in the walls of the Ishtar Gate of ancient Babylon made of molded brick with a glossy, colorful glaze. The lion was the symbol of Ishtar, the goddess of war and the protector of her people.

Large stone sculptures have been uncovered of lions with wings and a human head adorned as the king of Babylon. Their goddess Ishtar was sometimes shown standing on the back of a lion, or in the company of

45

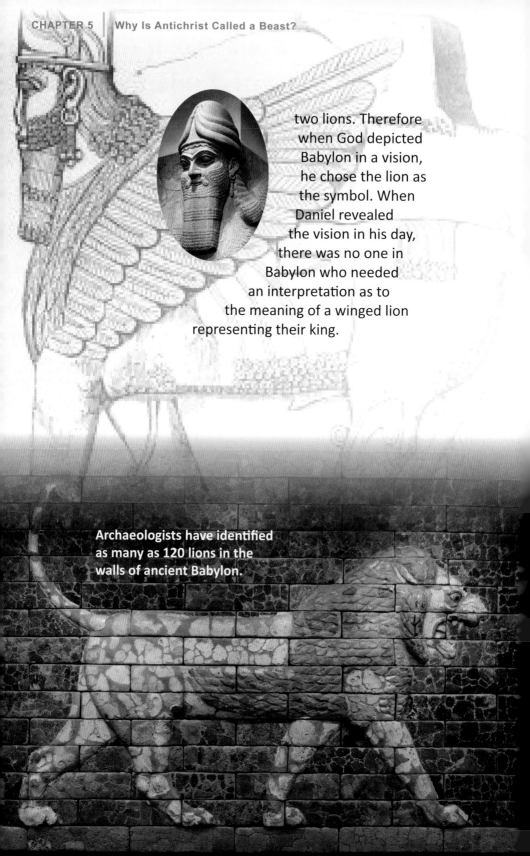

two lions. Therefore when God depicted Babylon in a vision, he chose the lion as the symbol. When Daniel revealed the vision in his day, there was no one in Babylon who needed an interpretation as to the meaning of a winged lion representing their king.

Archaeologists have identified as many as 120 lions in the walls of ancient Babylon.

The second beast, like to a bear.

The Second Beast
Medo-Persian Empire (538–330 BC)

5 And behold another beast, a second, like to a bear, and it raised up itself on one side, and it had three ribs in the mouth of it between the teeth of it: and they said thus unto it, Arise, devour much flesh.

The second beast was a bear that rose up with one shoulder higher than the other, and it had three ribs in its teeth. This beast is commanded to arise and devour much flesh. The phrase "raised up on one side" is symbolic of the Persians being more powerful than the Medes. The three ribs are symbolic of the three key victories the Medio-Persian Empire had: The defeat of King Croesus by Cyrus the Great and the conquest of Sardis, the capital of Lydia, in 547 BC; the conquest of Egypt by Cambyses in 525 BC; and the suppression of the Ionian Revolt by a number of cities in Asia Minor (Turkey) from 499–493 BC. In the vision, God commands this kingdom to take over and conquer more territory.

Why a bear? Scholars indicate that in Daniel's time the bears of Persia were some of the largest in the entire world.

God chose the swift leopard with wings to signify Alexander's swift victory

The Third Beast
Grecian Empire of Alexander the Great (331–31 BC)

6 After this I beheld, and lo another, like a leopard, which had upon the back of it four wings of a fowl; the beast had also four heads; and dominion was given to it.

The third beast is a leopard with four wings and four heads and represents the Greek Empire. God chose the swift leopard with wings to signify Alexander's swift victory, for he conquered all of Asia Minor (Turkey) in less than two years (334–333 BC) with 48,100 soldiers, 6,100 cavalrymen, and 120 ships. He defeated Darius III at the Battle of Issus in November of 333, taking control of the Persian Empire. After just seven years Alexander died, and his four generals divided the kingdom four ways—thus the four heads and four wings.

> The fourth kingdom... exceedingly dreadful...

The Fourth Beast
Roman Empire Consolidated (63 BC)

7 After this I saw in the night visions, and behold a fourth beast, dreadful and terrible, and strong exceedingly; and it had great iron teeth: it devoured and brake in pieces, and stamped the residue with the feet of it: and it was diverse from

all the beasts that were before it; and it had ten horns.

Daniel 7:19
Then I would know the truth of the **fourth beast,** which was diverse from all the others, exceeding dreadful, whose **teeth were of iron, and his nails of brass;** which devoured, brake in pieces, and stamped the residue with his feet;

Daniel 2:40
And the **fourth kingdom** (fourth beast) shall be strong as **iron: forasmuch as iron breaketh in pieces and subdueth all things: and as iron that breaketh all these, shall it break in pieces and bruise.**

He tells us that the fourth beast (the fourth kingdom) is diverse from the former three. Where they were symbolized by flesh-and-blood animals, this fourth kingdom is "strong as iron" with teeth of iron and nails of brass. It seems to be a mechanical beast so large that it steps on its enemies and crushes them. It totally devours and tramples down the former kingdoms. This beast is symbolic of the Roman Empire, which put to use the recent advance in steel construction in their chariots and implements of war.

The **ten horns refer to the ten barbarian nations that succeeded the Western empire** in the fourth and fifth centuries. The eleventh horn—the little horn—is antichrist who comes from one of the nations that comprised the old Roman Empire. And in the book of Revelation we learn that the ten horns also represent ten nations yet to coalesce around the coming antichrist.

Ten Horns of the Future

Daniel 7:23
Thus he said, The fourth beast shall be the fourth kingdom upon earth, which shall be diverse from all kingdoms, and shall devour the whole earth, and shall tread it down, and break it in pieces.

This statement is the interpretation of an angel from Daniel's perspective in 530 BC. The fourth kingdom from Daniel will be the Roman Empire.

Notice the head of the fourth kingdom is pictured as a beast, as was Nebuchadnezzar of Babylon, Medo-Persia, Greece, and now Rome. In the future **antichrist is going to establish himself as the head of the modern equivalent of the old Roman Empire, and is therefore referred to as a beast.**

24 And the ten horns out of this kingdom are ten kings that shall arise *[ten dominant nations from the old Roman Empire]*: **and another shall rise after them** *[antichrist]*; **and he shall be diverse from the first, and he shall subdue three kings** *[antichrist will gain control of three nations].*

New Testament Passages on the Beast

You will notice that the book of Revelation uses the word *beast* precisely as does the book of Daniel.

Read all of chapters 13 and 17 of Revelation and familiarize yourself with the use of the term *beast*. Following is a small sample of references.

Revelation 13:1–4

1 And I stood upon the sand of the sea, and saw a beast rise up out of the sea, having seven heads and ten horns *[matching the horns in Daniel (Daniel 7:7, 20, 24)]*, and upon his horns ten crowns, and upon his heads the name of blasphemy *[ten horns, ten crowns, ten heads—ten kings]*.
2 And the **beast which I saw was like unto a leopard, and his feet were as the feet of a bear, and his mouth as the mouth of a lion:** and the dragon gave him his power, and his seat, and great authority.
3 And I saw one of his heads as it were wounded to death; and his deadly wound was healed: and all the world wondered after the **beast.**
4 And they worshipped the dragon which gave power unto the **beast:** and they worshipped the **beast,** saying, Who is like unto the **beast?** who is able to make war with him? *[Read the entire chapter.]*

This is clearly a continuation of the same subject employing the same imagery as found in Daniel.

"And the ten horns out of this kingdom are ten kings that shall arise..."

Revelation 13:18
Here is wisdom. Let him that hath understanding count the number of the **beast:** for it is the number of a **man;** and his number is Six hundred threescore and six.

The beast is a man yet to arise out of the old Roman Empire.

The Answer to Our Question

So we have our answer as to why the Bible calls the antichrist a beast. It is to maintain the metaphor given to Daniel, thus creating an indelible link between the prophecies of Daniel and the prophecies of John in Revelation.

> *Here is wisdom. Let him that hath understanding count the* **number** *of the beast.*
>
> — *Revelation 13:18*

CHAPTER 6

Back to the Book of Daniel Concerning the Nature of Antichrist

Antichrist Arises from the Remnant of the Ancient Roman Empire

Daniel 7:8
I considered the horns, and, behold, there came up among them **another little horn,** before whom there were **three of the first horns plucked up by the roots:** and, behold, in this horn were **eyes like the eyes of man, and a mouth speaking great things.**

You will need to refresh your memory concerning this passage in its context. Speaking of the fourth beast (the fourth kingdom from Babylon), which is Rome, he tells us that the fourth beast has ten horns representing ten kings that shall arise, and there will be one more king that arises among the ten horns. He will pluck up three of the kings (nations) and will then speak great things against the Most High.

"...eyes like the eyes of man, and a mouth speaking great things."

55

- Antichrist arises from the remnant of the ancient Roman Empire.
- Antichrist defeats three nations (horns) as a means to gain power over the other seven.

End of the Tribulation

Daniel 7:9

I beheld till the thrones were cast down, and the **Ancient of days did sit,** whose garment was white as snow, and the hair of his head like the pure wool: his throne was like the fiery flame, and his wheels as burning fire.

We know from other passages that after antichrist declares himself to be God, he will continue for only 42 months until his throne is cast down and the Ancient of days sits on the throne to judge the nations (Matthew 25:31–32) and institute the Kingdom of Heaven in the millennium.

Considering Daniel 7:9, above, it is clear that Antichrist reigns until Jesus sits on the throne in the millennium.

Antichrist reigns until Jesus sits on the throne in the millennium.

At the Second Coming

Daniel 7:13
I saw in the night visions, and, behold, one like the **Son of man came with the clouds of heaven, and came to the Ancient of days,** and they brought him near before him.

The Millennial Reign of Christ upon the Earth

Daniel 7:14
And there was given him dominion, and glory, and a kingdom, that all people, nations, and languages, should serve him: his dominion is an everlasting dominion, which shall not pass away, and his kingdom that which shall not be destroyed.

Again it is clear that Daniel relates the events of the ten horns with the second coming of Christ.

Daniel Asks for Clarification

Daniel didn't understand what he saw in the prophetic vision, so he inquired of the angel and was given the interpretation. It is convenient to have a passage interpreted for us by an angel. It leaves no room for argument. Note the highlights in bold text.

Why Antichrist Is Called a Beast

So here is the interpretation we are looking for. It answers our question as to **why antichrist is called a beast.** In prophetic language, rulers of predatory kingdoms are represented as beasts. Antichrist is a beast that devours other kingdoms.

Daniel 7:17–27
**17 These great beasts, which are four, are four
kings, which shall arise out of the earth.
18 But the saints of the most High shall take the
kingdom, and possess the kingdom for ever, even
for ever and ever.**

Notice the issue is taking the kingdom.
Antichrist attempts to take the kingdom by force
(Matthew 11:12), but Jesus has more force, so he takes
the kingdom and gives it to the saints (Jews) "for ever
and ever."

Viewing the two consecutive verses above, and
taking note that the beasts are concurrent with the
saints taking the kingdom (Second Coming), we have
irrefutable confirmation of the interpretation that
antichrist is yet to arise as a beast—political leader in
the tradition of the beasts of Daniel whom we are told
are kings and kingdoms.

Daniel asked the angel for more information on the
fourth beast and the ten horns.

19 Then I would know the truth of the fourth beast,
which was diverse from all the others, exceeding
dreadful, whose teeth were of iron, and his nails
of brass; which devoured, brake **in pieces, and
stamped the residue with his feet;** [ancient Roman
Empire]
20 And of the ten horns that were in his head [ten
nations comprising the empire], and of the **other
which came up** [antichrist], and before whom three
fell; even of that horn that had eyes, and **a mouth
that spake very great things, whose look was more
stout than his fellows.**

Antichrist is going to be stronger than the other ten nations and Israel.

> **21** I beheld, and the same horn made war with the saints *[tribulation believers]*, and **prevailed against them;**

"I beheld, and the same horn made war with the saints *[tribulation believers]*, and prevailed against them;"

Antichrist will turn against the Jews when he declares himself to be God and they refuse to worship him. He will kill them everywhere, except the ones that flee into the wilderness where God feeds them as he did Israel in the wilderness under Moses (Revelation 12:14).

I cannot pass up the opportunity to mock the concept that Christians are going to endure the tribulation. According to this passage, for three and one-half years the "saints" will completely lose out to antichrist. He will thoroughly prevail against the saints. That would be a denial of the promise God made to the church: "Because thou hast kept the word of my patience, I also will keep thee from the hour of temptation, which shall come upon all the world, to try them that dwell upon the earth" (Revelation 3:10).

> **22 Until the Ancient of days came** [*Jesus at the Second Coming*]**, and judgment was given to the saints of the most High; and the time** [*as prophesied*] **came that the saints possessed the kingdom.**

This passage is not actually speaking of Christians. The "saints" are the Jews, and the kingdom they possess is not the kingdom of God; rather it is the **kingdom of heaven** promised to Abraham and Israel. If he were speaking of Christians, then we would be forced to conclude that at the present time Christian saints do not possess the kingdom. See my book *Eight Kingdoms* for more information on this subject.

Antichrist will be successful in his war against the nations, including Israel—until the Second Coming.

> **23 Thus he said, The fourth beast shall be the fourth kingdom upon earth,** which shall be diverse from all kingdoms, and **shall devour the whole earth,** and shall tread it down, and break it in pieces.

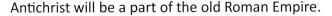

Antichrist will be a part of the old Roman Empire.

The reach of antichrist will extend to the whole earth.

> **24 And the ten horns out of this kingdom are ten kings that shall arise: and another shall rise after them; and he shall be diverse from the first, and he shall subdue three kings.**

Antichrist is the eleventh horn that shall arise from the same beast after the ten horns (kings) are well established.

Antichrist will be markedly different from the original beast that gave rise to the ten horns.

He will subdue three of the ten kings (nations) tipping the control to him.

> **25 And he shall speak great words against the most High, and shall wear out the saints of the most High, and think to change times and laws: and they shall be given into his hand until a time and times and the dividing of time.**

He will speak against the most High.

He will wear out the saints by pursuing them to the ends of the earth.

He will try to change the God-ordained prophetic calendar.

God will surrender the saints to antichrist for 1260 days.

Again I must pause to mock the concept of Christians enduring the tribulation. That would place God in the untenable position of turning believers over to antichrist for forty-two months.

26 But the judgment shall sit *[as a judge or jury is "seated"]***, and they shall take away his dominion, to consume and to destroy it unto the end.**

Antichrist's reign will end when the Judge is seated, and his helpers (angels and glorified saints returning on white horses at the end of the 1260 days) take away his dominion.

27 And the kingdom and dominion, and the greatness of the kingdom under the whole heaven, shall be given to the people of the saints of the most High *[Jews (meek) shall inherit the earth in keeping with promises made to Abraham and Israel]***, whose kingdom is an everlasting kingdom, and all dominions shall serve and obey him.**

After his judgment the kingdom will fall to the descendants of the saints.

All dominions will fall under the kingdom of heaven and will serve and obey Jesus Christ.

Antichrist Desecrates the Temple

Daniel 9:26–27

26 And after threescore and two weeks shall Messiah be cut off, but not for himself: and the people of the **prince that shall come** shall **destroy the city and the sanctuary; and the end thereof shall be with a flood,** and unto the end of the war desolations are determined.

27 And he shall confirm the covenant with many for **one week:** and in the **midst of the week he shall cause the sacrifice and the oblation to cease,** and for the overspreading of abominations he shall **make it desolate,** even until the consummation, and that determined **shall be poured upon the desolate.**

63

Daniel tells us,
"...he shall make it desolate..."

This passage is bursting with meaning.

- Antichrist (the prince that shall come) will destroy Jerusalem and the sanctuary.
- He will make a covenant with Israel for one week, a week being a week of 360-day times (2520 days), or a little over a month short of seven years.
- In the midst of the week (1260 days into the seven weeks of times) antichrist will prevent the Jews from offering sacrifices in the temple.
- Antichrist will cause the Jews to abandon the temple because he will perform an abomination by installing himself in the holy of holies, declaring that he is the God of the Jews (2 Thessalonians 2:3–4).
- The end will be with a flood. There was no flood in 70 AD when the temple fell to Rome, but there will be when antichrist persecutes the Jews during the tribulation (Revelation 12:15).

The End Shall Be with a Flood

This is another one of the hidden mysteries that the Scriptures reveal in passing. We cannot know for sure, but until we have more information it is safe to make assumptions based on a normal grammatical reading of the text.

> **Revelation 12:5–6, 14–17**
> **5 And she brought forth a man child, who was to rule all nations with a rod of iron: and her child was caught up unto God, and to his throne.**

This woman must be Israel, for the child who rules all nations with a rod of iron cannot be other than Jesus Christ (Revelation 2:27; 19:15). So this vision goes back to the birth of Christ and takes us down to the millennial kingdom.

The child "caught up" to God is the ascension of Christ after his resurrection.

> **6 And the woman fled into the wilderness, where she hath a place prepared of God, that they should feed her there a thousand two hundred and threescore days.**

The woman, Israel, flees into the wilderness below Jerusalem in an attempt to survive the persecution of antichrist. Jesus spoke of this even in Matthew 24:15–22 in very specific terms. It deserves reading.

God will preserve his people by supernaturally feeding them, apparently as he did in the wilderness under Moses—with manna.

> **14 And to the woman [Israel] were given two wings of a great eagle, that she might fly into the wilderness, into her place, where she is nourished**

for a time, and times, and half a time, from the face of the serpent.

The Jews "fly" into the wilderness. That passage would have seemed figurative 150 years ago, but today it is the most reasonable way for Jews to get into that inhospitable land. The Israeli military has several landing strips in the Sinai. It would be about a ten-minute flight.

Israeli survivors are nourished and fed for a time (360 days), and times (2 × 360 days), and a dividing of times (180 days)—1260 days in all; that is the last half of the seventieth week of Daniel.

15 And the serpent cast out of his mouth water as a flood after the woman, that he might cause her to be carried away of the flood.

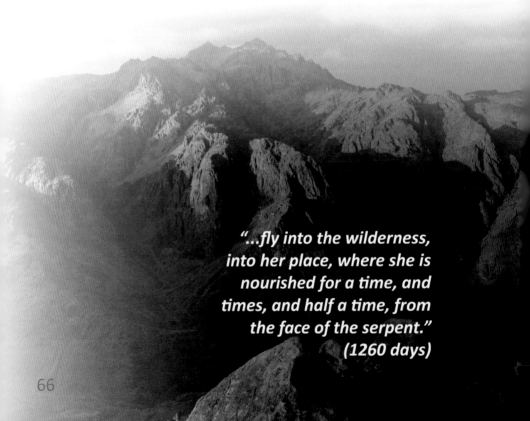

"...fly into the wilderness, into her place, where she is nourished for a time, and times, and half a time, from the face of the serpent." (1260 days)

The Jews will not be unarmed, and it would be at great loss to try to root them out of that impossible rugged terrain, so antichrist, under satanic guidance, sends a flood to wipe them out. How could that be? The wilderness around the Dead Sea is below sea level. The sea itself is 1388 feet below sea level—over a quarter of a mile. The Jews have had serious discussions about cutting a canal from the Red Sea to the Dead Sea and putting a lock on it so the Dead Sea can be refreshed and used for navigation. If they were hiding in that low area, by releasing water, a large portion of the wilderness around the sea could be flooded.

> **16 And the earth helped the woman, and the earth opened her mouth, and swallowed up the flood which the dragon cast out of his mouth.**

But God! Apparently the Jews will be in jeopardy, for God causes the earth itself to open up and assimilate the water, allowing the Jews time to escape to higher ground.

> **17 And the dragon was wroth with the woman, and went to make war with the remnant of her seed, which keep the commandments of God, and have the testimony of Jesus Christ.**

Since antichrist is unable to root out or drown the Jews in the wilderness, he turns to destroy those remaining in the nations.

CHAPTER 7

Return to New Testament Passages Revealing the Nature of Antichrist

Revelation 11:7 *[in reference to the two witnesses anointed by God]*
And when they shall have finished their testimony, the beast that **ascendeth out of the bottomless pit** shall **make war against them,** and shall **overcome them, and kill them.**

- Antichrist is called the beast.
- He came up from the bottomless pit.
- He will make war against the two Jewish witnesses, and overcome them, and kill them.

Revelation 20:4
And I saw thrones, and they sat upon them, and judgment was given unto them: and I saw the souls of them that were beheaded for the witness of Jesus, and for the word of God, and which had **not worshipped the beast, neither his image, neither had received his mark** upon their foreheads, or in their hands; and they lived and reigned with Christ a thousand years.

- He issues the imprint of a mark, number, or his name on everyone as a statement of their compliance and worship.
- He beheads those who will not receive his mark and worship him.

Revelation 13:3–7

3 And I saw one of his heads *[of the seven-headed beast]* as it were **wounded to death; and his deadly wound was healed:** and all the world wondered after the beast.

4 And they worshipped the dragon which gave power unto the beast: and they **worshipped the beast,** saying, Who is like unto the beast? Who is able to **make war** with him?

5 And there was **given unto him a mouth speaking great things and blasphemies; and power was given unto him to continue forty and two months.**

6 And he opened his mouth in **blasphemy against God,** to blaspheme his name, and his **tabernacle,** and **them that dwell in heaven.**

7 And **it was given unto him to make war with the saints, and to overcome them: and power was given him over all kindreds, and tongues, and nations.**

- The beast, antichrist, will suffer a deadly wound to his head, but he will recover.
- The world will be impressed by his recovery from seeming death and will worship him.
- God gives him the power to speak great things and to blaspheme.
- He will blaspheme the tabernacle.
- He will blaspheme those that dwell in heaven.
- He makes war against the saints (Israel) and anyone who refuses to comply.
- He will actually overcome all opposition.
  Evil wins during the tribulation. The two supernatural witnesses are killed. Heads roll. Jews abandon Israel and flee to the mountains. Antichrist is enthroned and worshipped as God.

- He continues 42 months (3½ years/1260 days/ time, times, and a half time).

Revelation 13:8
8 And **all that dwell upon the earth shall worship him,** whose names are not written in the book of life of the Lamb slain from the foundation of the world.

Antichrist will command universal worship.

Those whose names are written in the book of life of the Lamb will not worship antichrist on pain of death.

2 Thessalonians 2:8–12
8 And then shall that Wicked be revealed, whom the Lord shall consume with the spirit of his mouth, and shall destroy with the brightness of his coming: **9** Even him, whose coming is after the working of Satan with all power and signs and lying wonders, **10** And with all deceivableness of unrighteousness in them that perish; because they received not the love of the truth, that they might be saved.

11 And for this cause **God shall send them strong delusion, that they should believe a lie:**
12 That they all might be damned who believed not the truth, but had pleasure in unrighteousness.

This is a perspective-altering verse! While antichrist is attempting to deceive the world into believing him, Jesus is sending unbelievers a delusion to aid in their unbelief. God is not turning a screw in their brains so they helplessly swallow the antichrist's bait. The delusion is external. They see it with their hearts of unbelief and it makes it easier for them to be deceived. Again, God is not sending out a general cloud of unbelief. It is aimed at a certain group of people—those "who believed not the truth, but had pleasure in unrighteousness."

After the rapture there will be many people left on earth who had heard the truth of Christ before the rapture but did not believe it. Rather, they continued in the pleasure of unrighteousness.

Popular "Christian" novels and movies have painted an entirely false view of those "left behind." The only ones who cannot be saved after the rapture are those who thought they were Christians before and those who had heard the gospel but rejected it. They cannot because they will not. And they will not because they still love unrighteousness and they have Satan, antichrist, and God working to deceive them into missing Christ once again. Their inability lies in their unwillingness. And their unwillingness remains their choice. Those who would not choose Christ today would choose him for the wrong reasons when the sun is seven times hotter and the water has turned to blood.

Another Beast Assists Antichrist through His Universal Recognition as a Religious Leader

Revelation 13:11–17

11 And I beheld **another beast** coming up out of the earth; and he had two horns like a lamb, and he spake as a dragon.

This is another beast that does not spring from the same base as antichrist among the ten horns. He rises out of the earth, not the sea, being a product of the world at that time.

He comes looking like a lamb with two inoffensive little horns, but he speaks like Satan. The two horns represent consolidation of two powers into one personality, possibly the east and west division of structured Christianity—which would make him the Pope. Or it could be some yet-unimagined merging of Christianity and Judaism under one man.

> **12 And he exerciseth all the power of the first beast before him, and causeth the earth and them which dwell therein to worship the first beast, whose deadly wound was healed.**
> **13** And he **doeth great wonders,** so that he **maketh fire come down from heaven on the earth** in the sight of men,

This second beast exercises the authority of the first beast, indicating their close association and cooperation in the same endeavor. His role is to promote the antichrist to a place of divinity and worship in the world.

- The antichrist is assisted by a world-recognized religious leader who promotes worship of him.

"...by means of those miracles which he had power to do in the sight of the beast."

- This religious beast performs great miracles in the sight of the people, among which is his ability to call fire down from heaven as Elijah did.
- Antichrist is going to be wounded unto death, perhaps in an assassination attempt, but his wound will be healed as testimony to his supposed divinity.

14 And deceiveth them that dwell on the earth by the means of those miracles which he had power to do in the sight of the beast; saying to them that dwell on the earth, that they should make an image to the beast, which had the wound by a sword, and did live.
15 And he had power to give life unto the image of the beast, that the image of the beast should both speak, and cause that as many as would not worship the image of the beast should be killed.

The religious beast will thoroughly deceive the world with his miracles, adding credibility to his promotion of the worship of antichrist. He will cause an image of antichrist to speak. This would have been unthinkable until the twentieth century. Only now is it possible for everyone in the world to see and hear the image of a man speak. Furthermore the technology is current though not yet widely distributed that would allow the antichrist to monitor whether or not each person bows in front of the image.

The passage is amazing in its advanced technology. It says "that the image of the beast should both *[two things]* speak and cause . . . ." The image not only speaks, but the image itself causes that "as many as would not worship the image of the beast should be killed." Not only will the world's population be looking at the image, but the image will be looking at them. As they bow in front of their screens, the posture of each person will be analyzed by a computer and determination made as to compliance. The image will issue a capital sentence on all noncompliance.

- Antichrist will be worshipped by means of an image of himself, possibly because of his disfigurement.

Not only will the world's population be looking at the image, but it will be looking at them and the computer will be analyzing their compliance of worship.

- The religious beast will perform miracles attesting to the divinity of the first beast.
- Antichrist will impress the world with his recovery from a seemingly fatal wound to the head.
- His image will cause those who do not worship before it to be killed.

16 And he causeth all, both small and great, rich and poor, free and bond, to receive a mark in their right hand, or in their foreheads: 17 And that no man might buy or sell, save he that had the mark, or the name of the beast, or the number of his name.

18 Here is wisdom. Let him that hath understanding count the number of the beast: for it is the number of a man; and his number is **Six hundred threescore and six.**

The religious beast will cause everyone to display one of three things: (1) the mark—logo—of the beast, (2) the name of the beast, or (3) the numerical value of his name, which is 666. The identifying mark, name, or number will be placed in one of two places—the hand or the forehead.

There is no indication, as many have suggested, that each person is given an individual identification number, for the number given is "the number of his name"—666—which will be the same on everyone. Furthermore, the text indicates one of three possible identification marks, two of which have nothing to do with numbers—the mark or the name of the beast.

One who has the mark will not need the number or name. Likewise one who has the number of his name will not need the mark or name. Perhaps there will be different classes with different identifying symbols. Whether number, mark, or name, the purpose of each is to express loyalty to the beast. All those who receive any of these symbols will be damned by God without recourse. Those who reject the identifiers will be denied all participation in the economy.

The concept of a universal tattoo or microchip inserted in the hand lends itself to dramatic imaginations. It provides material for books and movies, and occasionally eliminates boredom. I have observed trends for seven decades and seen the "mark of the beast" go from a subdermal tattoo (after WWII), to a social security number, to a credit card, to a barcode on a can of creamed corn, to an implanted microchip, and next will be DNA markers expressed in numbers read with a hand scanner.

Some Christians treat the number 666 like it has magical powers for evil, avoiding it at all costs. Misinformation about the nature of the beast is actually preparing the world to be deceived by him. When the Rapture occurs, the world left behind will already be prepared for his "MARK."

Knowing that to be the value of his name, 666, will enable tribulation saints to identify antichrist. That may be an indication that he will come from one of the nations that express numbers by means of letters in the alphabet. Hebrew, Aramaic, Latin, and Greek come to mind.

The mark cannot be received until the man of sin, antichrist, has been revealed to the world. But the nature of the worship is present in all generation, as is the spirit of antichrist.

"...the sword shall be upon his arm, and upon his right eye: his arm shall be clean dried up, and his right eye shall be utterly darkened."

CHAPTER 8
Antichrist Wounded and Healed

We need to revisit in more detail the revelation that antichrist will be wounded to death and be healed.

Revelation 13:3
And I saw one of his heads as it were **wounded to death;** and his deadly **wound was healed:** and all the world wondered after the beast.

Zechariah 11:15–17 speaks of antichrist and is a parallel passage to Revelation 13:3. Reading the entire chapter will help establish a timeline, identifying the passage with antichrist. We will review several verses preceding the portion on antichrist to establish the timeframe of the prophecy. The amazing accuracy and chronological order of the several events predicted leaves no question that 15–17 is about antichrist.

Zechariah 11:10
And I took my staff, even Beauty, and cut it asunder, that I might break my covenant which I had made with all the people.

This is a prophecy of Jesus being cut off and of the 70 AD termination of God's Palestinian covenant with Israel as a result of their rejection.

Zechariah 11:12–17
12 And I said unto them, If ye think good, give me my price; and if not, forbear. So they weighed for my price **thirty pieces of silver.**

> **13** And the LORD said unto me, **Cast it unto the potter:** a goodly price that I was prised at of them. And I took the thirty pieces of silver, and **cast them to the potter in the house of the LORD.**

This is an amazingly detailed prophecy of Judas's betrayal of Christ. It is placed in the context of Christ (Beauty) being rejected and cut asunder. Matthew affirms that this passage was fulfilled in Judas (Matthew 27:9–10). He also tells us that before Zechariah wrote it down, Jeremiah spoke it.

Matthew's identification of this passage with Judas anchors the reader in a historical chronology of events.

Antichrist, the Foolish Shepherd

Israel, having rejected the true shepherd, Beauty, and purchasing his betrayal for thirty pieces of silver, will be given a foolish shepherd in antichrist.

> **15** And the LORD said unto me, **Take unto thee yet the instruments of a foolish shepherd.**
> **16** For, lo, **I will raise up** a shepherd in the land, which shall not visit those that be cut off, neither shall seek the young one, nor heal that that is broken, nor feed that that standeth still: but he shall **eat the flesh of the fat, and tear their claws in pieces.**
> **17** Woe to the **idol** *[as in an image]* **shepherd** that **leaveth the flock! the sword shall be upon his arm, and upon his right eye: his arm shall be clean dried up, and his right eye shall be utterly darkened.**

This is a fascinating prophecy of antichrist that provides us with background for understanding Revelation 13:3 (below) in connection with antichrist being wounded unto death but then healed.

- Antichrist is a foolish shepherd whom God raised up to be a source of judgment on Israel.
- Antichrist will have a clerical background, for he is said to be the shepherd that "leaveth the flock!" Perhaps he will be a rabbi or the like.
- He will use his position to bring destruction on Israel.
- As a shepherd, he is represented in an idol, an image to be venerated. This fits well with what we read of him in the book of Revelation.
- He will be wounded on his right side so that he loses sight in that eye and the use of his right arm.

Compare the above with Revelation 13:3. "And I saw one of his heads as it were **wounded to death;** and his deadly **wound was healed:** and all the world wondered after the beast."

- His recovery is a thing of wonder. It amazes the world.
- The image may be because of his appearance.
- He is called an idol shepherd.
- Make an image to the beast and cause it to speak (Revelation 13:15).
- He will imitate the resurrection of Christ.

The world will be shepherded by an idol. That seems like an appropriate judgment on a people who worship their electronics.

Make an Image to the Beast

As detectives, let us put all the clues together and see what they suggest, even if it is bizarre.

Antichrist is a shepherd who seeks worship. He likes to make public appearances with a display of wonders that impress people. As a public figure, he is exposed to an assassin who wounds him unto death. To everyone's amazement he recovers, but is blind in his right eye, and his right arm is dried up and totally useless. The damage must be devastating to affect both his eye and his arm from the same wound.

During the first three and one-half years of the seventieth week, antichrist deceives people through peace (Daniel 8:25), and Israel willingly signs a covenant with him (Daniel 9:24–27). He is so well liked that the people readily praise and worship him (Revelation 13:4). Then something causes antichrist to change from a peacemaker to a despot. Could it be that the assassination attempt and the disfigurement are what trigger the change? Read the two verses below and note the link between the wound and the image.

Revelation 13:14–15

14 And deceiveth them that dwell on the earth by the means of those miracles which he had power to do in the sight of the beast; saying to them that dwell on the earth, that they should make an image to the beast, which had the **wound by a sword, and did live.**

15 And he had power to give life unto the image of the beast, that the image of the beast should both speak, and cause that as many as would not worship the image of the beast should be killed.

At first they worship him directly, but after the deadly wound, they make an image of him—no doubt without the disfigurement—and cause the image to speak for him. So when they bow to worship, it will be before the speaking image. It well fits Daniel's description of him as the **idol** shepherd. The world will be shepherded by an idol. That seems like an appropriate judgment on a people who worship their electronics.

So as detectives we form a hypothesis that we cannot prove at this point, but we have enough information to paste it up on the wall in an order that allows us to consider it further. It will probably not be fully understood until it actually occurs, and I have no doubt that in that day the prophecy will be profound in its detail and literalness.

One Final, Bizarre Thought

If Jesus tarries another thirty years or so, Bible teachers will be pointing to androids that are capable of standing before an audience, looking and speaking exactly like the person after which they are fashioned. That would fit the prophecy to a P (P for prophecy)—make an image that speaks, one without disfigurement. Just a thought.

Antichrist's End

Revelation 19:19–20
19 And I saw the **beast,** and the kings of the earth, and their armies, gathered together to make **war against him that sat on the horse,** and against his army.
20 And the **beast was taken,** and with him the false prophet that wrought miracles before him, with which he deceived them that had received the mark of the beast, and them that worshipped his image. These both were **cast alive into a lake of fire burning with brimstone.**

Revelation 20:10
And the devil that deceived them was cast into the lake of fire and brimstone, where the beast and the false prophet are, and shall be tormented day and night for ever and ever.

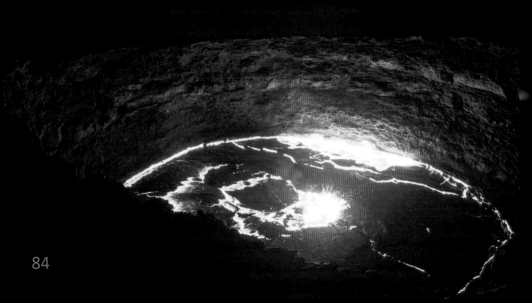

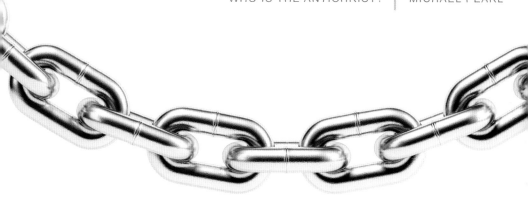

Antichrist is a **fake.** God let him (2 Thessalonians 2:11) out on a long chain to work his deception and to bring judgment on the world. But like Satan who spawned him, his place was always perdition, and to perdition he must return. In one final, desperate act of defiance, antichrist gathers his armies in the valley of Megiddo in an attempt to stave off the return of Jesus Christ to Jerusalem. Since Jesus and his followers all sit on horses, antichrist and his followers must think they will be no match against their own powerful implements of war. The outcome was never in doubt. It is of so little consequence that no mention is made of the battle. God didn't even brag about his defeat. It says they gathered together to battle and the next sentence says, "These both were cast alive into the lake of fire." And then we are told they "will be tormented day and night for ever and ever." That is forever on top of forever. So ends the short reign of the beast who would be God.

Key:

> **2 Thessalonians 2 says that God let Antichrist out on a long chain to work his deception and to bring judgment on the world.**

CHAPTER 9
Summary

This summary is a collection of bulleted points throughout the book. They have been arranged in chronological order as much as possible, providing a quick overview.

- There are many antichrists but just one end-time personality who will come.

- Antichrist existed prior to John's writing.

- He is the son of perdition—a product of perdition.

- Antichrist was not upon the earth at the time of John's writing.

- Yet he was in the bottomless pit (perdition) at the time of writing.

- He will ascend out of the bottomless pit at a later date.

- So it says he was, is not, and yet is, and shall be.

- His name is Wicked—the personification of all that is unholy.

- He is the man of sin.

- The nature of antichrist is a mystery of iniquity.

- He will be manifested to the world prior to the Second Coming.

- He will not come until there is a general falling away from the faith.

- Satan enables him to come into the world.

- He was counted among the believers as a shepherd and went out from them.

- He was not a true believer.

- Antichrist will have a clerical background, for he is said to be a shepherd that "leaveth the flock!" Perhaps he will be a rabbi or the like.

- Antichrist is a foolish shepherd whom God raised up to be a source of judgment on Israel.

- He comes as a peacemaker.

- He is a false prophet.

- He speaks great things.

- He understands dark secrets—mysteries.

- Satan gives him the power of deception.

- God sends a strong delusion on those who did not believe prior to the rapture so they will believe the antichrist's lies and be damned.

- He comes with ALL deceivableness in regard to those who perish.

- He will deceive many.

- He is filled with the spirit of error.

- He abides not in the doctrine of Christ.

- He denies that Jesus Christ came in the flesh.

- He denies the Father and the Son, attempting to acknowledge the Father without the Son.

- He is the beast of Daniel and Revelation.

- He is a political ruler known as the "little horn."

- Antichrist is the eleventh horn that shall arise from the same beast after the ten horns (kings) are well established.

- Antichrist will be markedly different from the original beast that gave rise to the ten horns.

- He will be the eighth of seven kings.

- Antichrist is a beast in the tradition of powerful world leaders.

- Antichrist arises from the remnant of the ancient Roman Empire.

- He conquers three other kingdoms before gaining control of all ten.

- Antichrist is going to be stronger than the other ten nations.

- The reach of antichrist will extend to the whole earth.

- He will be in a position to form policy.

- He will prosper in his endeavors.

- He will practice his agenda.

- He will cause craft to prosper.

- He will attempt to change times and laws.

- He will magnify himself in his heart.

- Satan enables him to possess all kinds of power witnessed by public signs and wonders, and lying miracles.

- He will display mighty power.

- He will make a covenant with Israel.

- After three and one-half years, he will install himself in the holy of holies in the temple in Jerusalem declaring that he is God.

- He will commit the abomination of desolation.

- The abomination will cause the Jews to cease offering sacrifices in the temple.

- He will use his position to bring destruction on Israel.

- He will wear out the saints of the Most High.

- He will persecute the Jews that remain on the earth after the rapture and cause them to flee into the wilderness.

- God will surrender the saints to antichrist for 1260 days.

- Antichrist will be successful in his war against the saints (Jews) until the Second Coming.

- He will make war against the two Jewish witnesses, and overcome them, and kill them.

- He makes war against anyone who refuses to comply.

- He will actually overcome all opposition. Evil wins during the tribulation. The two supernatural witnesses are killed. Heads roll. Jews abandon Israel and flee to the mountains. Antichrist is enthroned and worshipped as God.

- He will destroy Jerusalem and the sanctuary.

- He devours and breaks in pieces.

- His level of destruction is amazing.

- He is a king of fierce countenance.

- He stands against the Prince of Peace.

- He shall speak words against the Most High.

- He exalts himself above all gods or objects of worship.

- He will sit in the Jewish temple in Jerusalem as a way of demonstrating that he is God.

- He exalts himself above the god of every religion and above every object of worship.

- He will blaspheme the tabernacle.

- He will blaspheme those that dwell in heaven.

- Antichrist is going to be wounded unto death, perhaps in an assassination attempt, but his wound will be healed as testimony to his supposed divinity.

- As a result of the wound, he loses sight in his right eye, and his right arm is withered and useless.

- Antichrist will impress the world with his recovery from a seemingly fatal wound.

- His recovery will imitate the resurrection of Christ.

- The false prophet will make an image to the beast and cause it to speak on his behalf.

- Antichrist will be worshipped by means of the image of himself universally displayed.

- Thus he is called an idol shepherd.

- God gives him the power to speak great things and to blaspheme.

- **He issues the imprint of a mark,** number, or his name on everyone as a statement of their compliance and worship.

- The numerical value of his name is 666.

- Some will display a mark that signifies antichrist.

- Everyone will display one of the three signifiers in honor to antichrist or be denied participation in the economy.

- The image of the beast enforces compliance.

- He beheads those who will not receive his mark and worship him.

- Those whose names are written in the book of life of the Lamb will not worship antichrist on pain of death.

- Antichrist is assisted by a world-recognized religious leader who promotes worship of him.

- This religious beast performs great miracles in the sight of the people, among which is his ability to call fire down from heaven as Elijah did.

- Antichrist reigns up until Jesus sits on the throne in the millennium.

- He continues 42 months (3½ years/1260 days/time, times, and a half time).

- He will be broken by Jesus Christ without Christ so much as lifting his hand.

- The end will be with a flood. There was no flood in 70 AD when the temple fell to Rome, but there will be when antichrist persecutes the Jews during the tribulation (Revelation 12:15).

- Antichrist's reign will end when the Judge is seated, and his helpers (angels and glorified saints returning on white horses at the end of the 1260 days) take away his dominion.

- All dominions will fall under the kingdom of heaven and will serve and obey Jesus Christ.

- The kingdom of heaven suffers violence under antichrist, but the violent Christ takes the kingdom by force at his second coming.

- Jesus will cast antichrist into the lake of fire.

- After his judgment the meek shall inherit the earth.

"He that hath an *ear,*
LET HIM
hear what the
Spirit *saith*
UNTO THE *churches.*"

— *Revelation 2:29*